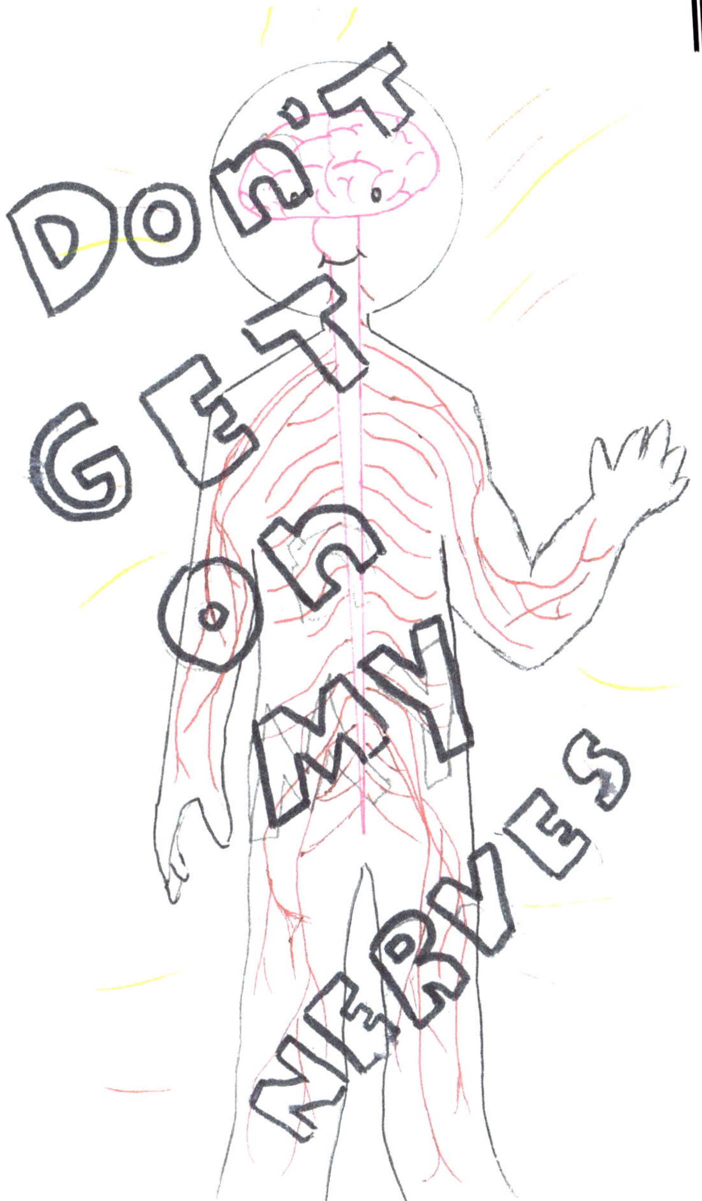

Written by

Sherry Blair

Illustrated by

Jayden Blair

Don't Get on My Nerves

First Edition

Hardcover ISBN: 978-1-68515-363-2
Paperback ISBN: 978-1-68515-364-9

Dedication

This book is dedicated
to Craig and Jordan Blair
for believing in me.

Love you all!

Hi! My name is Mr. Nervous Nelly, and sometimes my nerves get the best of me. You see, the nervous system has two main parts: the central nervous system, also known as the CNS for short, and the peripheral nervous system, also known as the PNS for short. We will start with the CNS and what it does in the body. The central nervous system has two main parts: the brain and the spinal cord. The spinal cord is made up of vertebrae.

Well, everyone knows what the brain is, but do you know what vertebrae are? The vertebrae make up the spinal column, which is your backbone. It starts from your neck and goes all the way down to your tail bone or bottom. It helps protect the spinal cord, and it helps Mr. Nervous Nelly move and maintain balance. People like Mr. Nervous Nelly have thirty-three vertebrae in their bodies, but that can change. One can have thirty-three or thirty-seven. Some people can have extra, or some can have fewer vertebrae in their bodies.

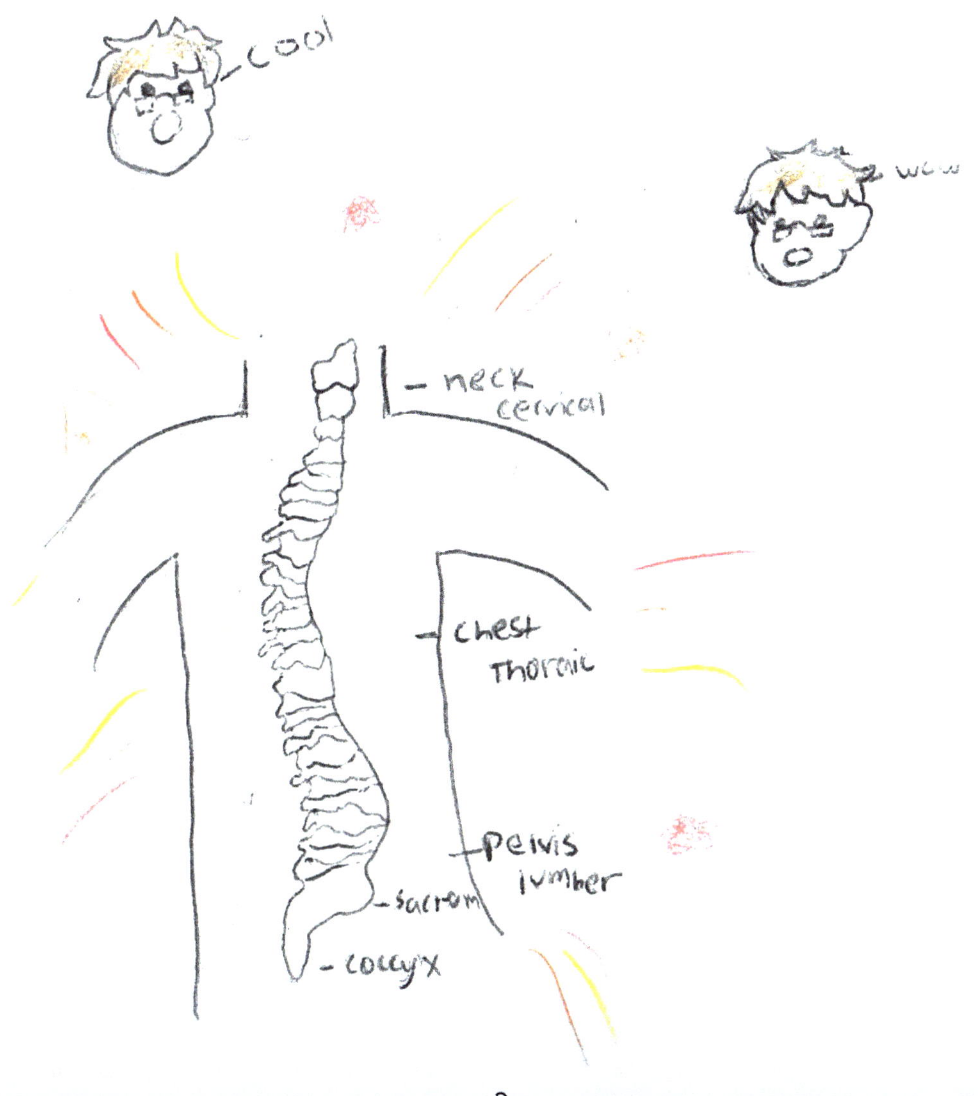

Now that we understand the CNS and what it does, we can further break it down. The CNS has four parts that help the body maintain daily functions. The cerebrum is the front part of the brain, and it controls voluntary movement and conscious processes such as memory, emotions, thought, reason, language, and voluntary muscle activity. Mr. Nervous Nelly is a little stressed out because he's going to the gym to work out, and he's consciously using the muscles in his body to move so he can work out. Mr. Nervous Nelly feels a bit stressed, which is one of his emotions because he does not like to work out. The emotions he feels include reason, thought patterns, and more. These voluntary actions come from this part of the brain, the cerebrum.

The next part of the CNS is called the cerebellum. Mr. Nervous Nelly is starting to get annoyed. Mr. Nervous Nelly needs his nerves to move and function while exercising, and the nerves are getting on his nerves. The cerebellum is located near the brain stem, and it is the largest part in the back of the brain cord. It is responsible for many things, but some of the primary responsibilities are motor skills such as balance, coordination (like walking), posture, the way a person sits, and memory.

The cerebellum is responsible for movement, and walking is one example of an activity that requires timing. An example is walking, like putting one foot in front of the other, which needs timing. Mr. Nervous Nelly's exercise routine includes many different movements requiring timing, such as jumping, running, and boxing. Boxing requires hand movements that are timed, just like walking.

The third part of the CNS is the brain stem. It has many structural parts: the medulla oblongata, pons, midbrain, and finally, the spinal cord, which is connected to the brain stem. The medulla oblongata is to the back region of the brain stem. It is connected to the spinal cord, which is known as your backbone. The pons is very good. It is responsible for sending memories to parts of the brain, involving breathing, taste, eye movement, and more. The midbrain is primarily responsible for the movement of the eye, hearing, and body movement.

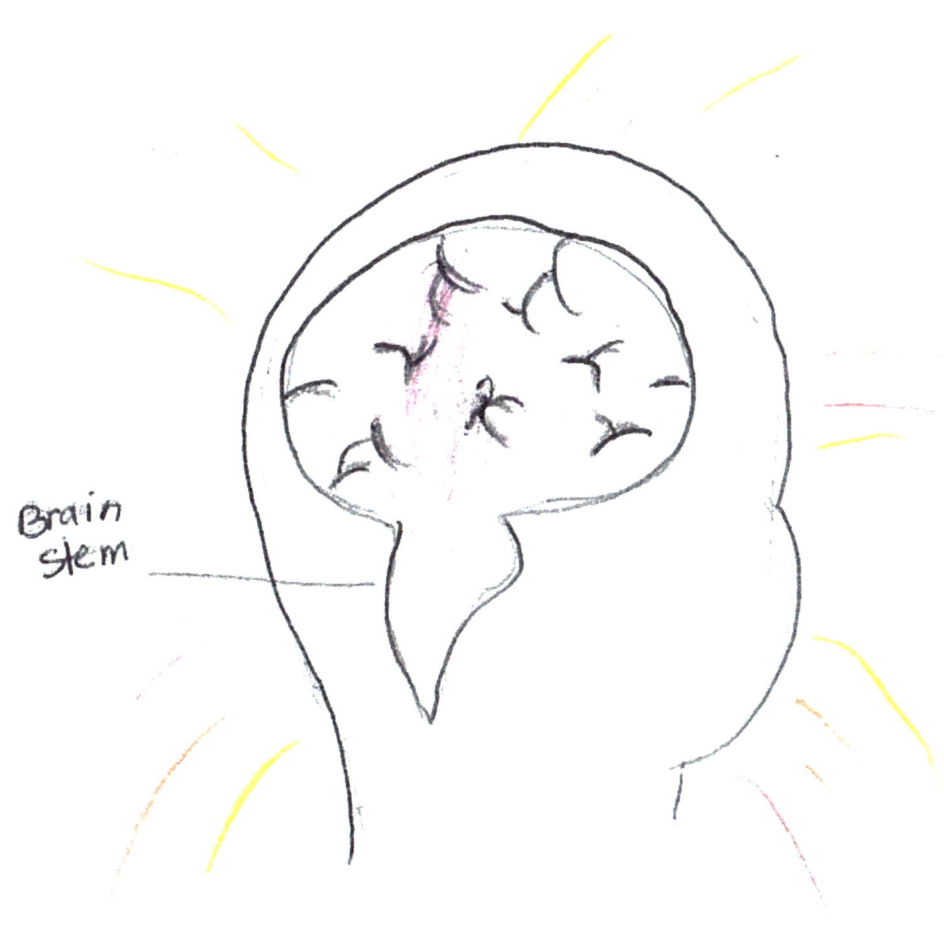

Even though Mr. Nervous Nelly is stressing about his workout, he is starting to realize that he needs his nerves to survive. You see, the brain stem is responsible for sending messages that can hold daily functions like the heart rate (which means how fast or slow Mr. Nervous Nelly's heartbeats are), breathing, and swallowing.

Another part of the central nervous system is the diencephalon, which is located deep in the brain. The diencephalon is responsible for sending messages to all parts of the body. This means that the diencephalon receives signals from nerves and then sends the signals out into the human body to function efficiently. Mr. Nervous Nelly is starting to appreciate the nerves in his body and is making sure that the nerves are not getting the best of him. The most important parts of the diencephalon are the hypothalamus, epithalamus, thalamus, subthalamus, and many more. All of these play a part in sending messages to make our bodies work efficiently.

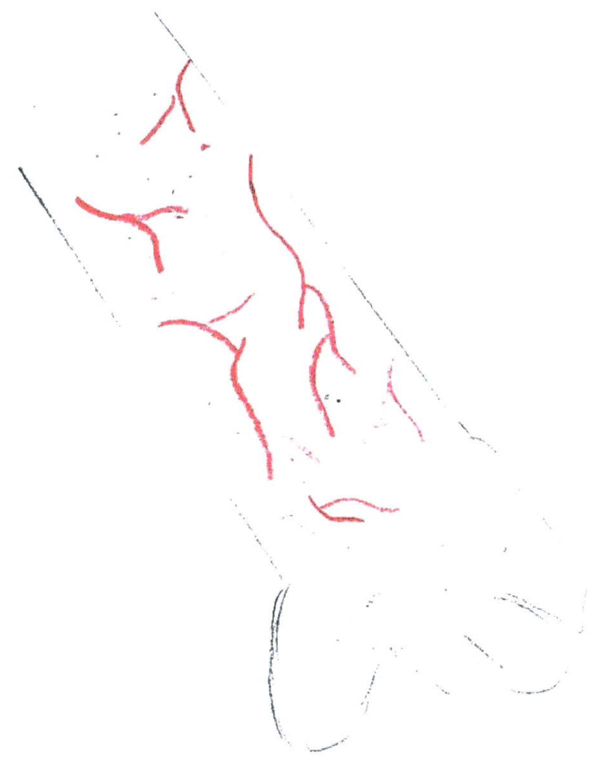

Now that we are finished describing some of the key points of the CNS, we will now describe some of the key points of the PNS and how it works. The peripheral nervous system has two branches.

We will start with the autonomic nervous system. The autonomic nervous system maintains involuntary bodily functions. It involves actions or things you cannot control or do on your own, such as the heartbeat, food digestion, and breathing.

The structures of the autonomic nervous system are the sympathetic system, parasympathetic system, and enteric system. The sympathetic system regulates the flight-or-fight system, which controls how you would react in situations. "Fight or flight" simply means that you would stay and fight the situation or leave the situation (flight) when something wrong happens. Mr. Nervous Nelly's peripheral system also helps him digest his food and much more.

Mr. Nervous Nelly is not nervous anymore about anything in life. In fact, he has a better outlook on things, and he is putting his nerves to good use. The next branch of the PNS is the somatic nervous system responsible for voluntary muscle movement. "Voluntary" means it is a movement you can control.

The system functions by carrying nerve signals back and forth to the CNS, skeletal muscles, and sensory organs. The somatic nervous system is part of the efferent nerves, which are the motor nerves, and the afferent nerves, which are responsible for the senses.

Mr. Nervous Nelly is so happy about his nerves that he would like to describe how the sympathetic nervous system works. The sympathetic nervous system is part of the autonomic nervous system, which includes the PNS. Once again, the sympathetic nervous system's primary function is to activate the flight-or-fight response. This is when bad stuff is occurring or happening, and your mind and body immediately send out hormones through the body to flee or stay and fight the situation.

The nervous system is now Mr. Nervous Nelly's favorite system because the parasympathetic nervous system is responsible for relaxing the body and slowing down any energy functions the body has by using hormones. Today, thanks to the parasympathetic nervous system, Mr. Nervous Nelly's day is good because he is relaxing. Some examples of the body resting are sleeping, sitting, or doing whatever makes the body chill. The body rest when a person relaxes after a busy activity like exercising.

Neuroglia cells are also called glial cells, and they are part of the nervous system. The structure of the neuroglia cells is the myelin, which supports and protects the framework of the nervous system. There are four types of neuroglia cells: astrocytes, ependyma, oligodendrocytes, and microglia. They are all responsible for doing specific jobs.

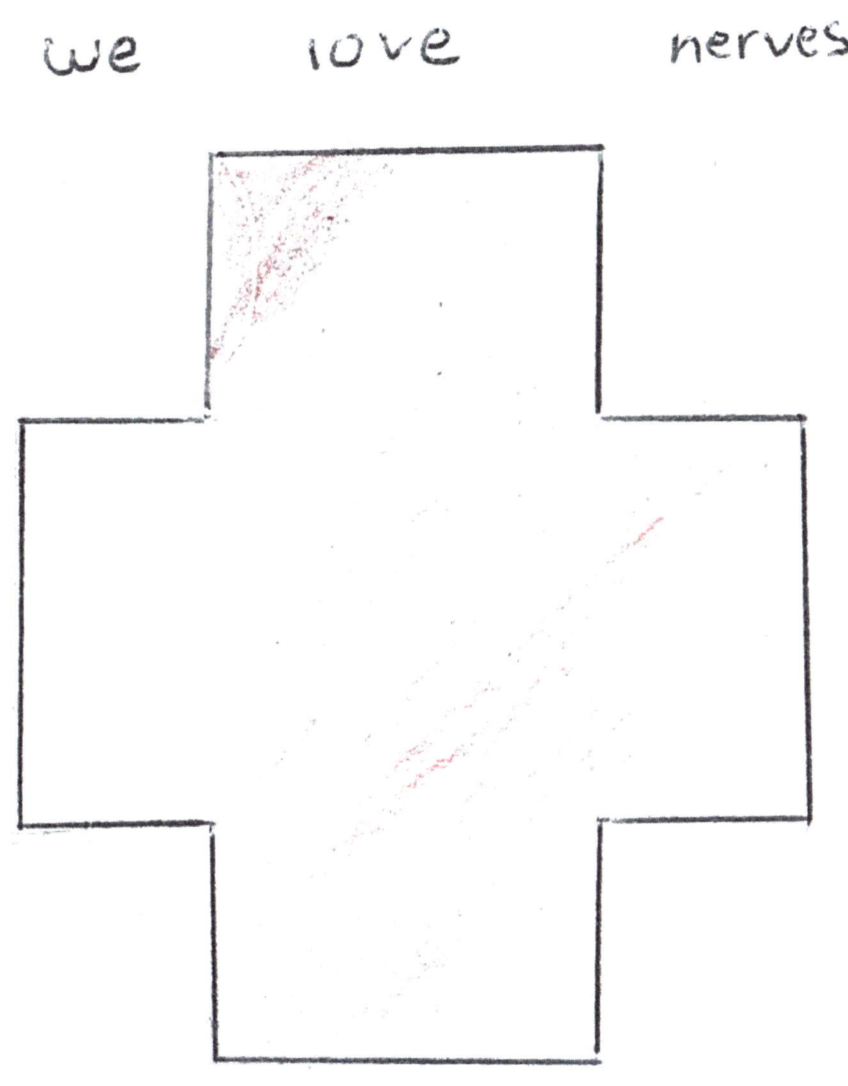

Mr. Nervous Nelly knows that if any of your nerves in the CNS or PNS are damaged or injured during physical functions, you should stop, or major pain will continue throughout the body. Either way, the CNS and PNS are very, very important in the human body because they are responsible for many important daily functions.

So we are at the end of our explanation of the CNS and the PNS. Mr. Nervous Nelly is pleased to have all these things to help his body function and do so many things so easily.

Lastly, we have neurons, and they are responsible for transmitting signals throughout the body. Neurons have long, narrow, rodlike extensions that extend out from a cell body. Neurons use chemical and electrical signals to communicate to the brain and the body. This is how we can eat, feel pain, walk, and do so many more things, including physical activities that the human body can do.

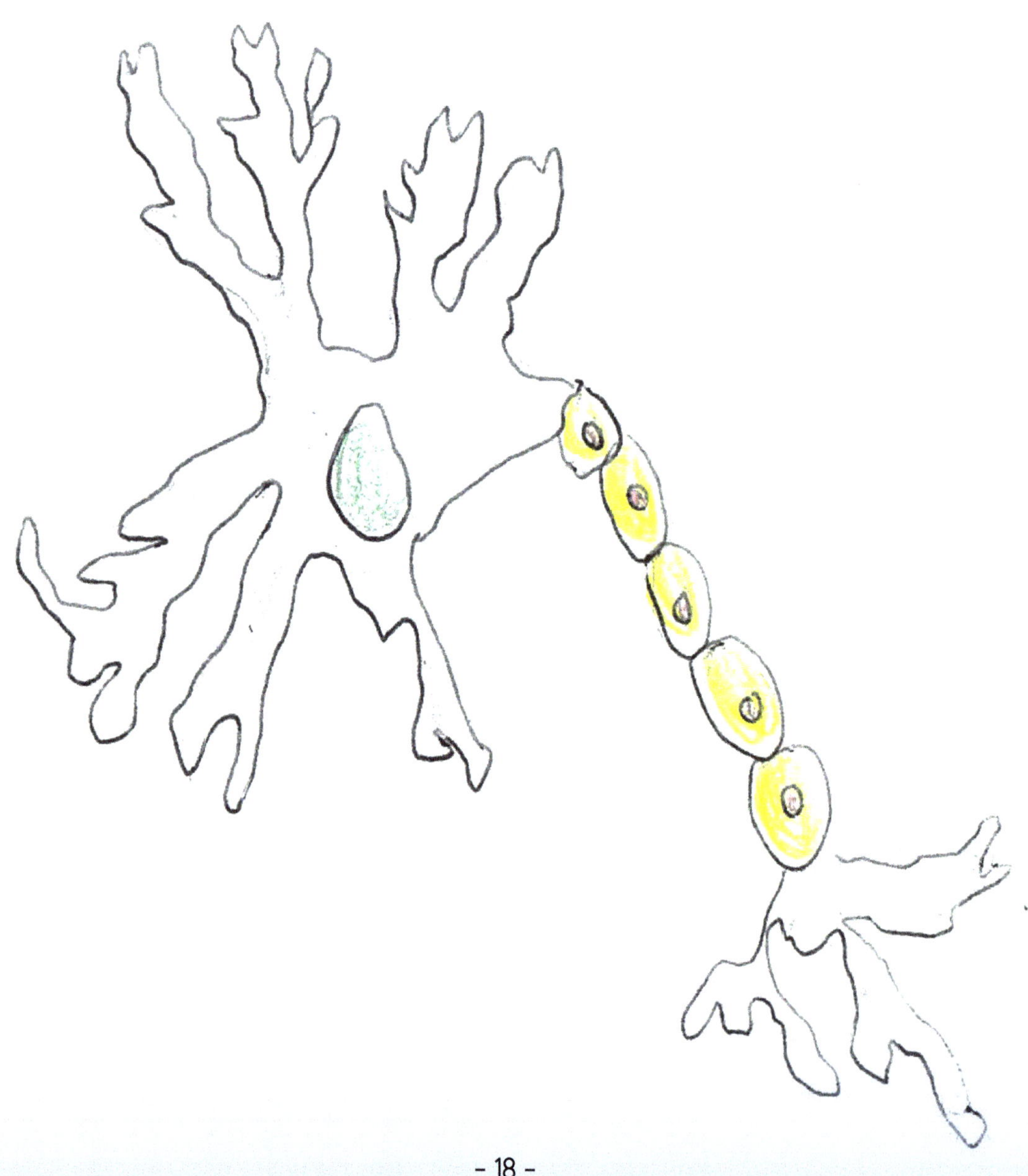

Without neurons, the human body would be unable to move or do any physical activity. The average neuron structure consists of dendrites, a nucleus, an axon, a cell body, and more. Mr. Nervous Nelly has realized how vital neurons and the central and peripheral nervous systems are and is very happy and grateful to have them in his body.

REFERENCES:

1. Thau L, Reddy V, Singh P. Anatomy, Central Nervous System. [Updated 2021 May 8]. In: StatPearls [Internet. Treasure Island (FL): StatPearls Publishing; 2021 Jan. Available from: https://www.ncbi.nlm.nih.gov/books/NBK542179/

2. https://www.healthline.com/health/cerebellum#function

3. https://med.libretexts.org/Bookshelves/Anatomy_and Physiology/Book%3A_Anatomy_and_Physiology_(Bound less)/11%3A_Central_Nervous_System/11.6%3AThe_Di encephalon/11.6A%3A_Functions_of_the_Diencephalon

4. Waxenbaum JA, Reddy V, Varacallo M. Anatomy, Auto nomic Nervous System. [Updated 2021 Jul 29]. In: Stat Pearls [Internet]. Treasure Island (FL): StatPearls Pub lishing; 2021 Jan-. Available from: https://www.ncbi.nlm.nih.gov/books/NBK539845/

5. Alshak MN, M Das J. Neuroanatomy, Sympathetic Ner vous System. [Updated 2021 Jul 26]. In: StatPearls [Internet]. Treasure Island (FL): StatPearls Publishing; 2021 Jan-. Available from: https://www.ncbi.nlm.nih.gov/books/NBK542195/

6. https://en.wikipedia.org/wiki/Glia

7. https://www.healthline.com/health/neurons#parts

www.ingramcontent.com/pod-product-compliance
Ingram Content Group UK Ltd.
Pitfield, Milton Keynes, MK11 3LW, UK
UKHW062006290726
14090UKWH00022B/1421

9 781685 153649